Beginning Piano Solo

Christmastime

8 Holiday Classics Arranged for Beginners

ISBN 978-1-4768-1261-8

HAL•LEONARD® CORPORATION
7777 W. BLUEMOUND RD. P.O. BOX 13819 MILWAUKEE, WI 53213

For all works contained herein:
Unauthorized copying, arranging, adapting, recording, Internet posting, public performance,
or other distribution of the printed music in this publication is an infringement of copyright.
Infringers are liable under the law.

Visit Hal Leonard Online at
www.halleonard.com

Contents

ALL I WANT FOR CHRISTMAS IS MY TWO FRONT TEETH

Words and Music by
DON GARDNER

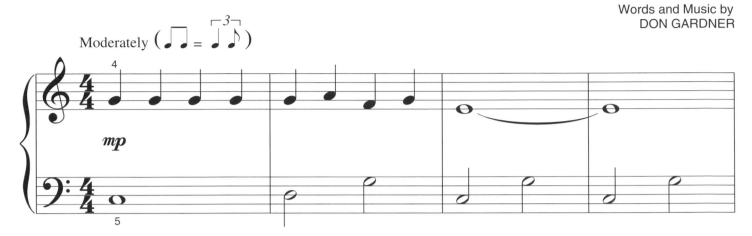

© 1946 (Renewed) WB MUSIC CORP.
This arrangement © 2012 WB MUSIC CORP.
All Rights Reserved   Used by Permission

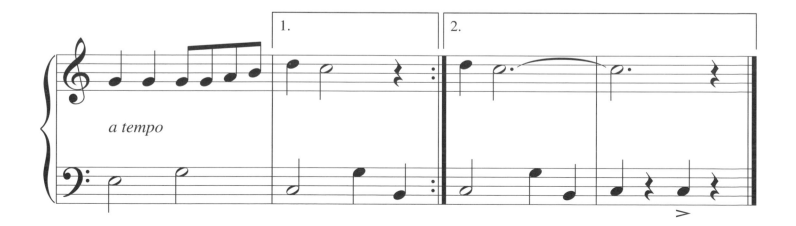

DO YOU HEAR WHAT I HEAR

Words and Music by
NOEL REGNEY and GLORIA SHAYNE

Moderately

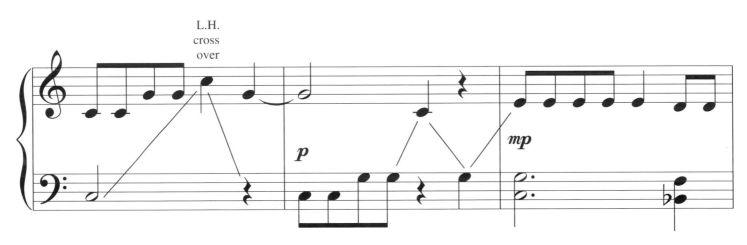

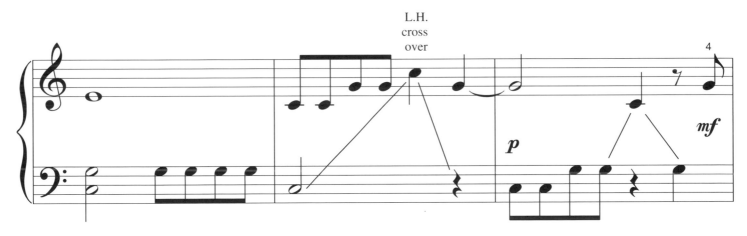

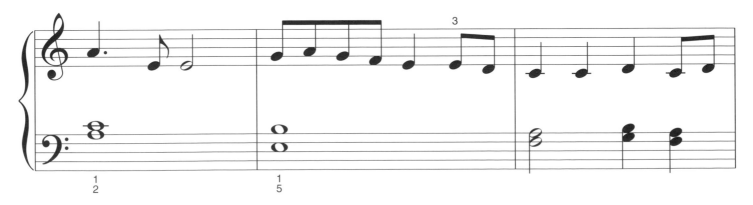

Copyright © 1962 (Renewed) by Jewel Music Publishing Co., Inc. (ASCAP)
This arrangement Copyright © 2012 by Jewel Music Publishing Co., Inc.
International Copyright Secured   All Rights Reserved
Used by Permission

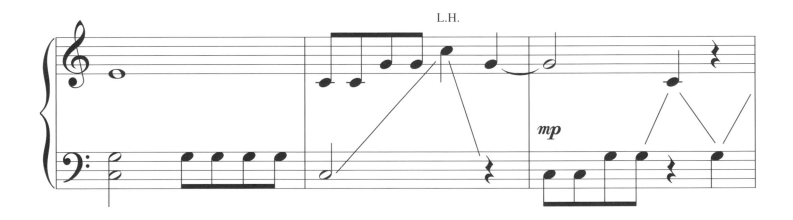

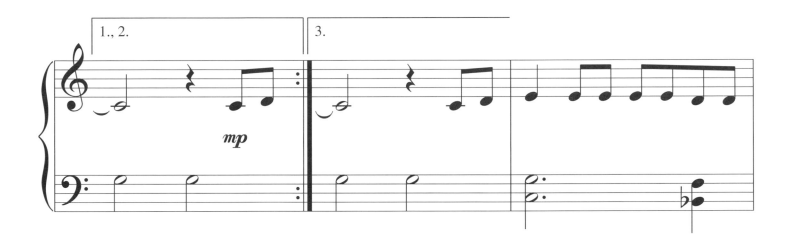

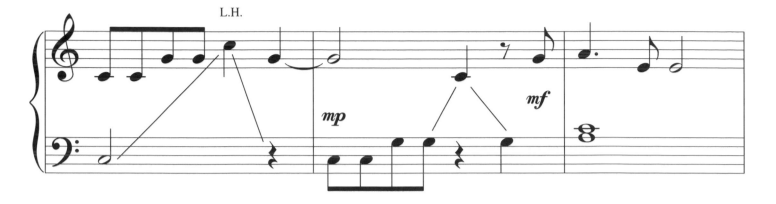

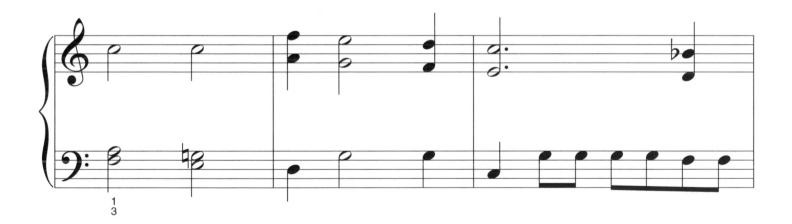

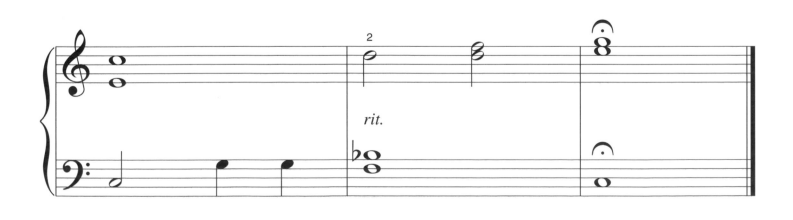

CAROLING, CAROLING

Words by WIHLA HUTSON
Music by ALFRED BURT

TRO - © Copyright 1954 (Renewed) and 1957 (Renewed) Hollis Music, Inc., New York, NY
This arrangement TRO - © Copyright 2012 Hollis Music, Inc.
International Copyright Secured
All Rights Reserved Including Public Performance For Profit
Used by Permission

HERE COMES SANTA CLAUS
(Right Down Santa Claus Lane)

Words and Music by
GENE AUTRY and OAKLEY HALDEMAN

Brightly

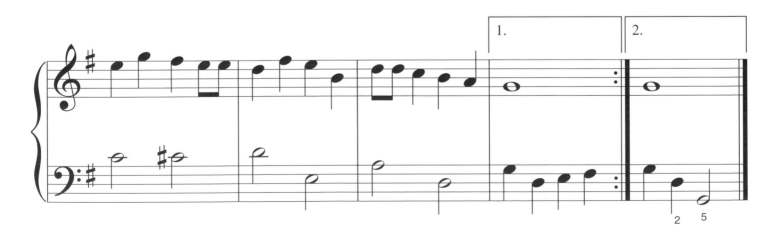

© 1947 (Renewed) Gene Autry's Western Music Publishing Co.
This arrangement © 2012 Gene Autry's Western Music Publishing Co.
All Rights Reserved   Used by Permission

SLEIGH RIDE

Music by LEROY ANDERSON
Words by MITCHELL PARISH

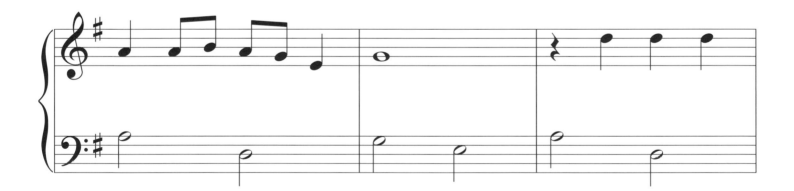

© 1948, 1950 (Copyrights Renewed) WOODBURY MUSIC COMPANY and EMI MILLS MUSIC, INC.
This arrangement © 2012 WOODBURY MUSIC COMPANY and EMI MILLS MUSIC, INC.
Worldwide Print Rights Administered by ALFRED MUSIC PUBLISHING CO., INC.
All Rights Reserved   Used by Permission

To Coda

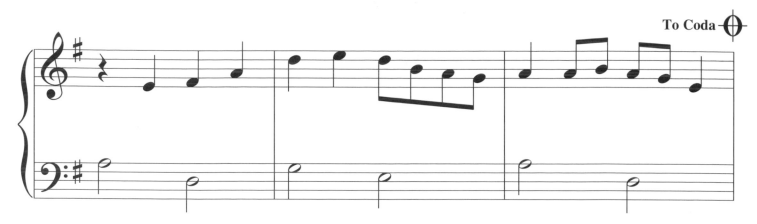

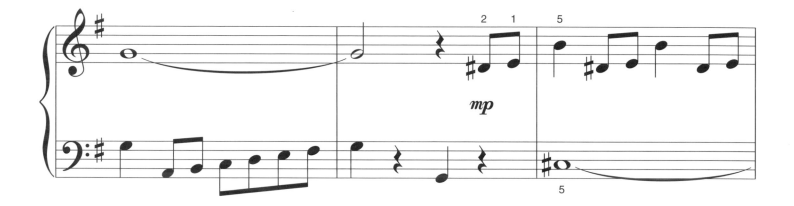

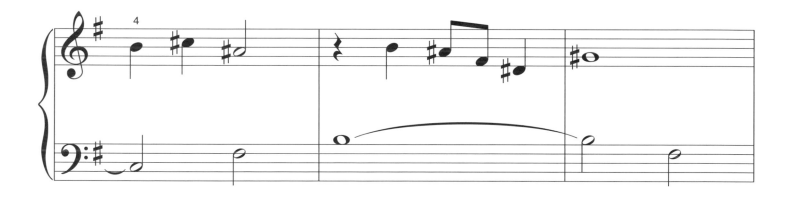

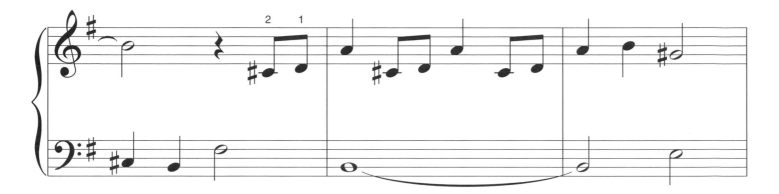

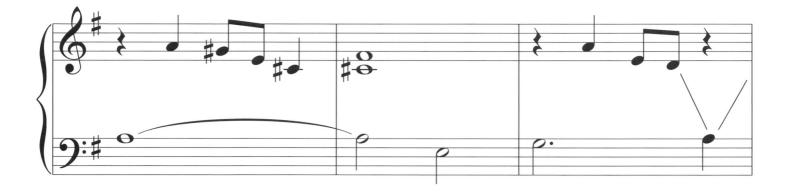

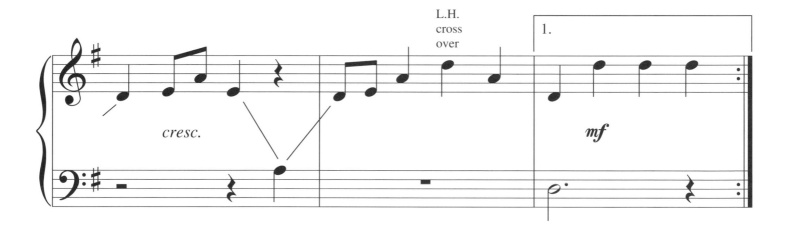

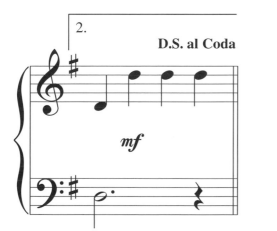

I'LL BE HOME FOR CHRISTMAS

Words and Music by
KIM GANNON and WALTER KENT

Slowly

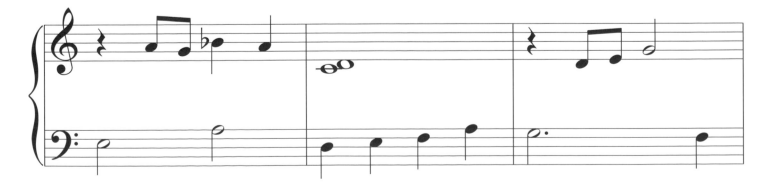

© Copyright 1943 by Gannon & Kent Music Co., Inc., Beverly Hills, CA
Copyright Renewed
This arrangement © Copyright 2012 by Gannon & Kent Music Co., Inc.
International Copyright Secured   All Rights Reserved

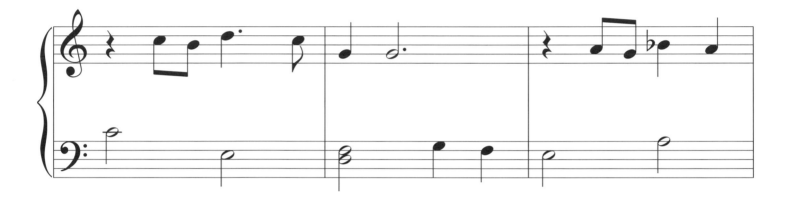

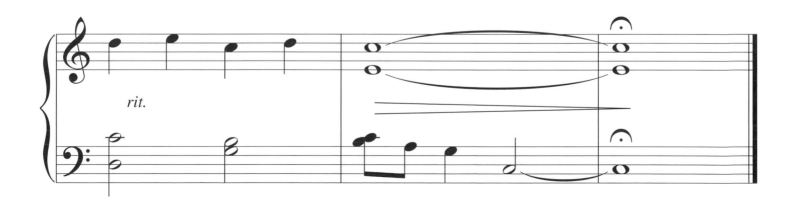

THE LITTLE DRUMMER BOY

Words and Music by HARRY SIMEONE,
HENRY ONORATI and KATHERINE DAVIS

Moderately

© 1958 (Renewed) EMI MILLS MUSIC, INC. and INTERNATIONAL KORWIN CORP.
This arrangement © 2012 EMI MILLS MUSIC, INC. and INTERNATIONAL KORWIN CORP.
Worldwide Print Rights Administered by ALFRED MUSIC PUBLISHING CO., INC.
All Rights Reserved   Used by Permission

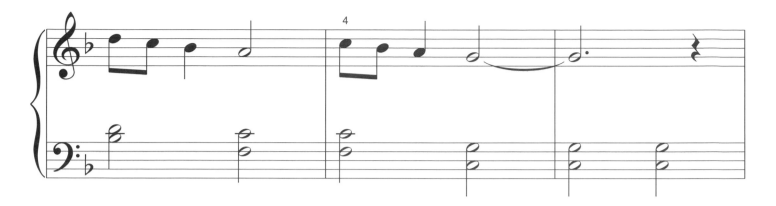

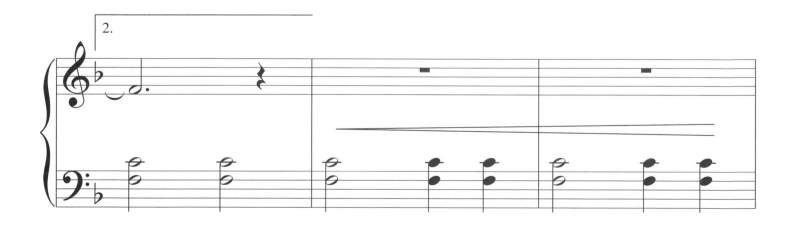

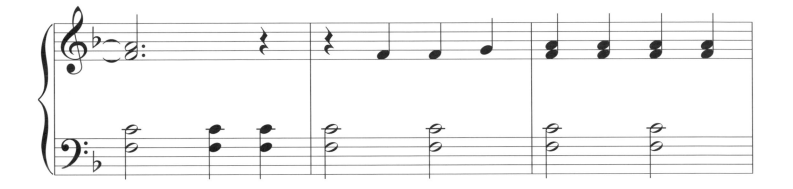

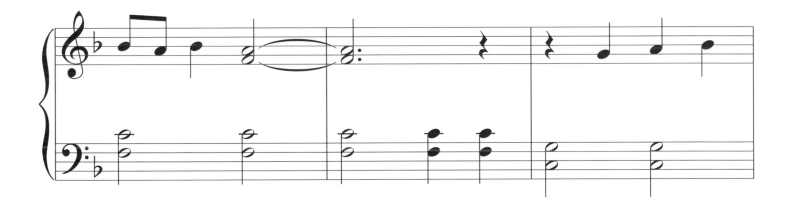

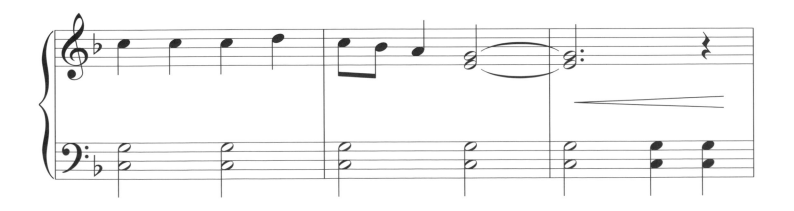

THE MOST WONDERFUL TIME OF THE YEAR

Words and Music by
EDDIE POLA and GEORGE WYLE

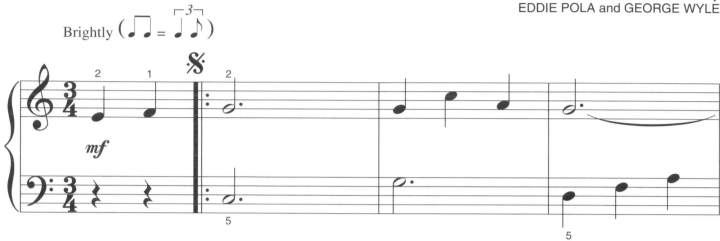

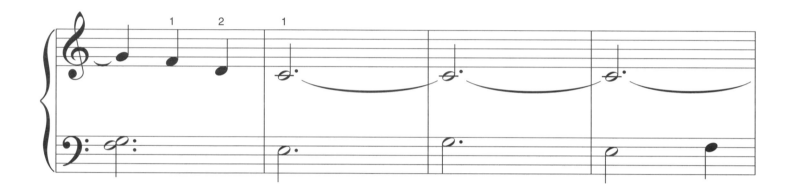

Copyright © 1963 Barnaby Music Corp.
Copyright Renewed
This arrangement Copyright © 2012 Barnaby Music Corp.
Administered by Lichelle Music Company
International Copyright Secured   All Rights Reserved

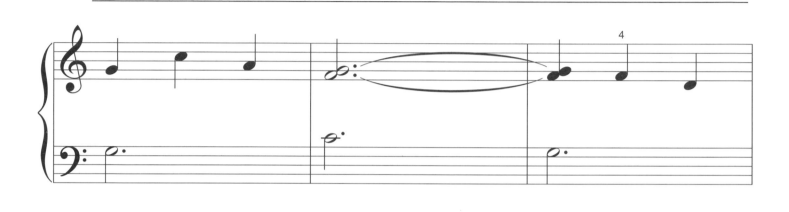

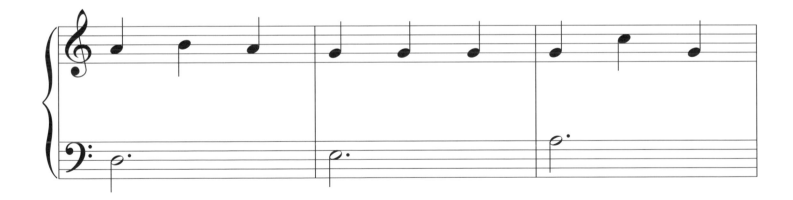

D.S. al Coda

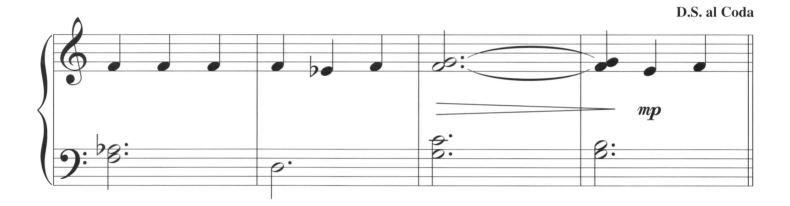

mp

CODA

8va

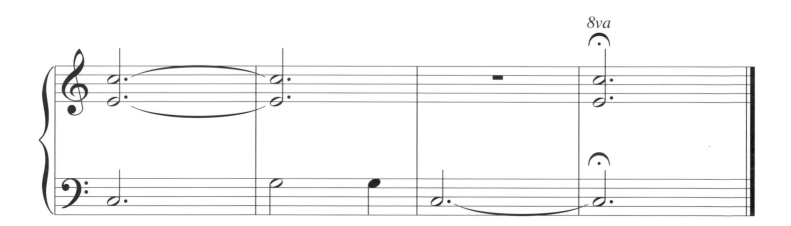

Christmas Collections
from Hal Leonard
All books arranged for piano, voice & guitar.

All-Time Christmas Favorites – Second Edition
This second edition features an all-star lineup of 32 Christmas classics, including: Blue Christmas • The Chipmunk Song • The Christmas Song • Frosty the Snow Man • Here Comes Santa Claus • I Saw Mommy Kissing Santa Claus • Jingle-Bell Rock • Let It Snow! Let It Snow! Let It Snow! • Merry Christmas, Darling • Nuttin' for Christmas • Rockin' Around the Christmas Tree • Rudolph the Red-Nosed Reindeer • Santa, Bring My Baby Back (To Me) • There Is No Christmas like a Home Christmas • and more.
00359051...$14.99

The Best Christmas Songs Ever – 4th Edition
69 all-time favorites are included in the 4th edition of this collection of Christmas tunes. Includes: Auld Lang Syne • Coventry Carol • Frosty the Snow Man • Happy Holiday • It Came Upon the Midnight Clear • O Holy Night • Rudolph the Red-Nosed Reindeer • Silver Bells • What Child Is This? • and many more.
00359130...$21.99

The Big Book of Christmas Songs – 2nd Edition
An outstanding collection of over 120 all-time Christmas favorites and hard-to-find classics. Features: Angels We Have Heard on High • As Each Happy Christmas • Auld Lang Syne • The Boar's Head Carol • Christ Was Born on Christmas Day • Bring a Torch Jeannette, Isabella • Carol of the Bells • Coventry Carol • Deck the Halls • The First Noel • The Friendly Beasts • God Rest Ye Merry Gentlemen • I Heard the Bells on Christmas Day • It Came Upon a Midnight Clear • Jesu, Joy of Man's Desiring • Joy to the World • Masters in This Hall • O Holy Night • The Story of the Shepherd • 'Twas the Night Before Christmas • What Child Is This? • and many more. Includes guitar chord frames.
00311520...$19.95

Christmas Songs – Budget Books
Save some money this Christmas with this fabulous budget-priced collection of 100 holiday favorites: All I Want for Christmas Is You • Christmas Time Is Here • Feliz Navidad • Grandma Got Run Over by a Reindeer • Happy Holiday • I'll Be Home for Christmas • Jesus Born on This Day • Last Christmas • Merry Christmas, Baby • O Holy Night • Please Come Home for Christmas • Rockin' Around the Christmas Tree • Some Children See Him • We Need a Little Christmas • What Child Is This? • and more.
00310887...$12.99

The Definitive Christmas Collection – 3rd Edition
Revised with even more Christmas classics, this must-have 3rd edition contains 127 top songs, such as: Blue Christmas • Christmas Time Is Here • Do You Hear What I Hear • The First Noel • A Holly Jolly Christmas • Jingle-Bell Rock • Little Saint Nick • Merry Christmas, Darling • O Holy Night • Rudolph, the Red-Nosed Reindeer • Silver and Gold • We Need a Little Christmas • You're All I Want for Christmas • and more!
00311602...$24.95

Essential Songs – Christmas
Over 100 essential holiday favorites: Blue Christmas • The Christmas Song • Deck the Hall • Frosty the Snow Man • A Holly Jolly Christmas • I'll Be Home for Christmas • Joy to the World • Let It Snow! Let It Snow! Let It Snow! • My Favorite Things • Rudolph the Red-Nosed Reindeer • Silver Bells • and more!
00311241...$24.95

The Muppet Christmas Carol
Matching folio to the blockbuster movie featuring 11 Muppet carols and eight pages of color photos. Bless Us All • Chairman of the Board • Christmas Scat • Finale - When Love Is Found/It Feels like Christmas • It Feels like Christmas • Marley and Marley • One More Sleep 'Til Christmas • Room in Your Heart • Scrooge • Thankful Heart • When Love Is Gone.
00312483...$14.95

Tim Burton's The Nightmare Before Christmas
This book features 11 songs from Tim Burton's creepy animated classic, with music and lyrics by Danny Elfman. Songs include: Jack's Lament • Jack's Obsession • Kidnap the Sandy Claws • Making Christmas • Oogie Boogie's Song • Poor Jack • Sally's Song • This Is Halloween • Town Meeting Song • What's This? • Finale/Reprise.
00312488...$12.99

Ultimate Christmas – 3rd Edition
100 seasonal favorites: Auld Lang Syne • Bring a Torch, Jeannette, Isabella • Carol of the Bells • The Chipmunk Song • Christmas Time Is Here • The First Noel • Frosty the Snow Man • Gesù Bambino • Happy Holiday • Happy Xmas (War Is Over) • Hymne • Jesu, Joy of Man's Desiring • Jingle-Bell Rock • March of the Toys • My Favorite Things • The Night Before Christmas Song • Pretty Paper • Silver and Gold • Silver Bells • Suzy Snowflake • What Child Is This • The Wonderful World of Christmas • and more.
00361399 ....$19.95

FOR MORE INFORMATION, SEE YOUR LOCAL MUSIC DEALER, OR WRITE TO:

HAL•LEONARD® CORPORATION
7777 W. BLUEMOUND RD. P.O. BOX 13819 MILWAUKEE, WI 53213
Complete contents listings available online at www.halleonard.com
PRICES, CONTENTS, AND AVAILABILITY SUBJECT TO CHANGE WITHOUT NOTICE.

0611